Contents

T0385910

Welcome to Rise and Shine Towers

1 Trace and match.

Hi! I'm Dexter.

I'm Bruno.

My name's Mia.

My name's Elena.

1

2

3

4

2 🖍 💬 Trace and color. Then ask and answer.

1 2 3 4 5

6 7 8

9 10

Tell me!
How old are you?
I'm 4.

What's your favorite color? Tell a friend.

Extra time?

3 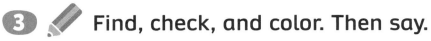 Find, check, and color. Then say.

It's a pencil.
It's green.

I can shine!

4 Draw and write for you. Then say.

Hi! My name is
_____.

I'm _____.

color me

Old toys, new toys

Let's review! SB p6 Find and color.
Then trace and say.

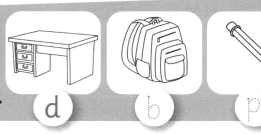

d   b   p

1 Trace and match.

ball

train

robot

teddy bear

car

doll

elephant

tablet

Tell me!
Look at my
new words.
Match and
color.

a

Toys

b

School
things

Say the words in alphabetical order.

**Extra
time?**

1 Listen and circle.

1 (a)   b

2 a   b

3 a   b

4 a   b

2 Read and check (✓) or put an ✗.

1 It's a teddy bear. [✗]

2 It's a robot. [ ]

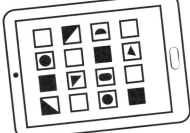

3 It's a tablet. [ ]

4 It's a car. [ ]

I can shine!

3 ✏ Color a toy in Activity 2. Write. Then tell a friend.

It's a _____.

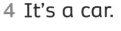 color me

Write your favorite toy word. _____

1 SB p12–13 ➡ **Which toy is new? Look and check (✓).**

2 ✏ **Find and color. Then circle.**

Let's imagine!
It's a doll /
an elephant.

I can shine!

3 ✏ **Draw. Then say.**

And you? What's
your favorite toy
at school?

color me

Rate the story and tell a friend. ☆☆☆

**Extra
time?**

1 Read and trace. Then circle.

It's a doll / teddy bear.

It's big / small.

Let's build!
What is it?

2 Follow, find, and number. Then say.

1
2
3
4

It's new. ☐   It's old. ☐

It's green. ☐   It's a teddy bear. **1**

Think of an old toy you have. Draw and share with a friend.

Extra
time?

1 🎧 1.13 ✏️ Listen and color.

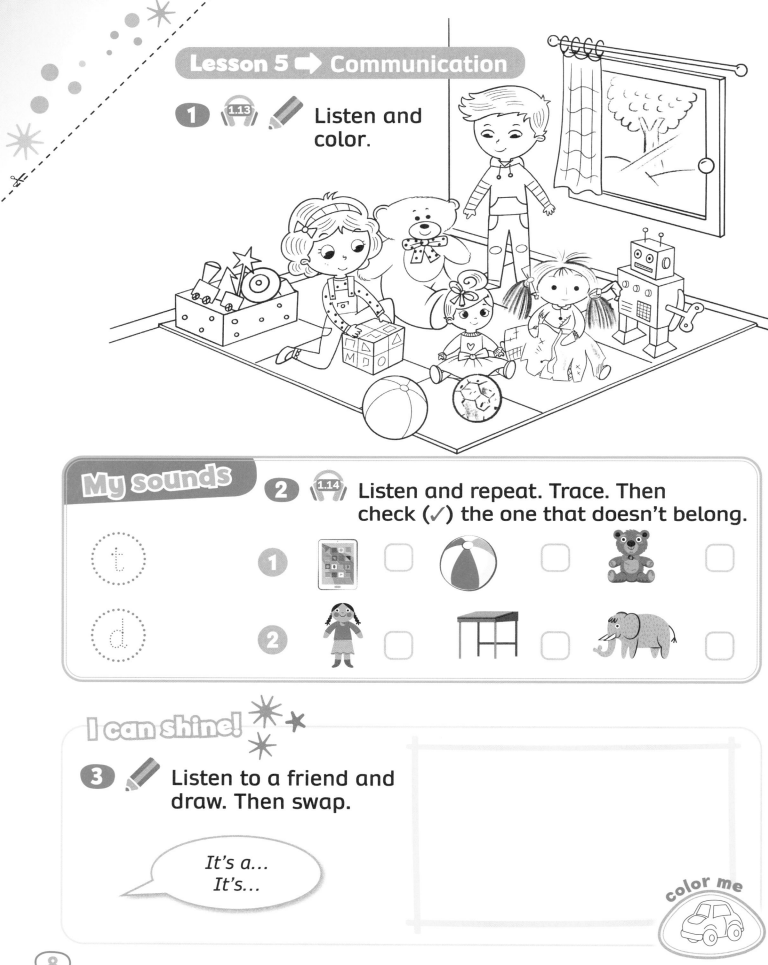

My sounds

2 🎧 1.14 Listen and repeat. Trace. Then check (✓) the one that doesn't belong.

t

d

1

2

I can shine!

3 ✏️ Listen to a friend and draw. Then swap.

It's a...
It's...

color me

1 Find and circle the one that doesn't belong. Then say.

It's a new doll.

• New •

• Old •

I can shine!

Think and share
Do you share your toys?

2 Look and write. Then role-play.

What's this?

It's a _____.

What toys do your friends share with you? Talk with a friend.

Extra time?

1 Trace and number.

It's...

a ball. ☐   a tablet. ☐

a car. ☐   a doll. ☐

a teddy bear. ☐   a robot. ☐

a train. ☐   an elephant. 1

1 2 3 4 5 6 7 8

2 ✏️ 💬 Choose and check (✓). Draw and color. Then tell a friend.

It's...

new. ☐   small. ☐

old. ☐   big. ☐

It's...

green. ☐   yellow. ☐

blue. ☐   red. ☐

> It's a big car.
> It's red.

What's this? It's a _ _ _ _ _ box.

Extra time?

3 ✏️ ✂️ 💬 Stick, draw, and color.
Then play the game.

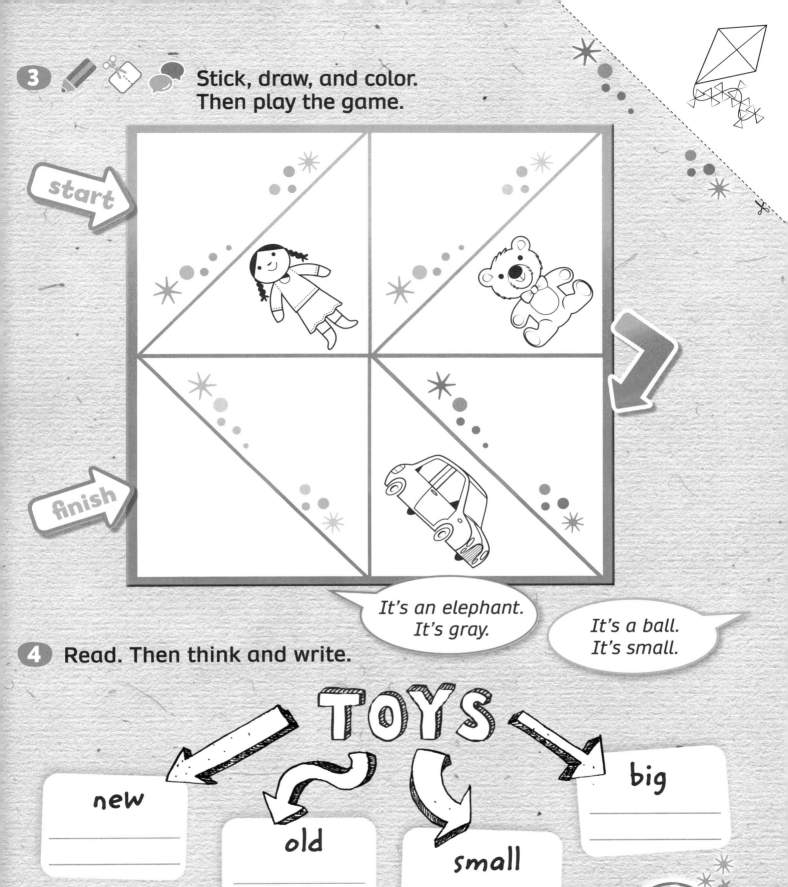

start

finish

It's an elephant.
It's gray.

It's a ball.
It's small.

4 Read. Then think and write.

TOYS

new

old

small

big

Make a toy box. Then show and tell your family.

Home-school
link

11

All kinds of families

Let's review! SB p10–11 ➡ Find and trace. Then say.

b   t   c

1 Trace and match.

brother

sister

mom

dad

grandma

grandpa

aunt

uncle

Tell me!
Look at my new words. Match and color.

Toys

Family

Say the words in alphabetical order.

Extra time?

1 **Listen and match.**

This is my family.

1   **2**   **3**   **4**

a **b** **c** **d**

2 **Read. Then look at Activity 1 and number.**

This is my grandma, my grandpa, and my sister. ☐

This is my mom, my dad, and my brother. ☐

I can shine!

3 ✏ **Draw someone in your family. Write. Then tell a friend.**

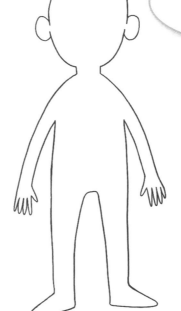

This is my _____.

color me

Write your favorite family word. _____

Extra time?

13

1 SB p22–23 Who is in Bruno's family? Look and check (✓).

1  ☐

2  ☐

3  ☐

2 Follow. Then circle.

Let's imagine!
I have a brother / an aunt.

I can shine!

3 🖊 Draw. Then say.

And you? Who's in your family?

color me

Rate the story and tell a friend. ☆☆☆

Extra time?

1 **Read and trace. Then circle.**

1 I have a
hamster /
bird.

2 I have a
cat / bird.

3 I have a
fish / cat.

2 **Match and say.**

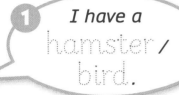

1  **2**  **3**  **4**

Let's build!
I have a brother.

a  **b**  **c**  **d**

I have a sister.   I have a grandma.   I have a cat.   I have a mom.

Think of a pet for you. Draw and share with a friend.

Extra time?

1 🎧 *2.13* Listen and number.

 a

 b

 c

 d 1

My sounds

2 🎧 *2.14* Listen and repeat. Trace. Then match.

c

g

I can shine!

3 💬 Check (✓) for you. Then tell a friend.

I have a...
And you?

color me

1 Read and match. Then say.

This is for my cousin.

 **1**
 **2**
 **3**
 **4**

a neighbor

b cousin

c friend

d pet

I can shine!

Think and share
Do you help your friends and family?

2 ✏️ Draw and write. Then role-play.

This is for my _____.

Extra time?

Who do you help in your family? Tell a friend.

1 Trace. Then number for Dexter.

Bruno is my brother.

This is my...

mom. [1]	grandma. ☐	aunt. ☐	
dad. ☐	grandpa. ☐	uncle. ☐	sister. ☐

2 Look and read. Check (✓) or put an ✗ for you. Then tell a friend.

I have a bird and a cat.

I have a hamster and a fish.

	🦜	🐱	🐹	🐟
1	✓	✓	✗	✗
2	✗	✗	✓	✓
3 Me				

Who's this? It's ___ ___ ___ ___ ___ ___ Felipe.

Extra time?

3 ✏️ 💬 **Stick, draw, and color. Then complete the family tree.**

This is my grandpa.

I have a hamster.

4 **Read. Then think and write.**

Me

Family

Friends

Pets

Make a picture album page. Then show and tell your family.

Review 1 Important to me

1 🖊 Color and say.

It's a train.

2 🎧 2.19 💬 Listen and number. Then ask and answer.

a · b · c `1` · d · e

Who's this?

This is my...

What's this?

It's a...

3 Connect the dots. Then read, trace, and circle.

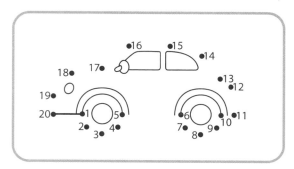

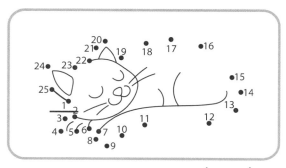

1 It's a train / car.

2 This is my cat / bird.

4 Read and trace. Then check (✓) for you.

I have...

a new bike.   an old plane.   a big cat.   a small fish.

5 ✏️ Think of a toy to play with. Draw, write, and say.

Let's play with the _____.

Mini-project

6 ✏️ Think of a toy to give to your best friend. Draw and write.

This is for you, _____.

It's a _____.

Time to shine!

7 ✏️ Read and color.

1 I can write toy words.

2 I can write family words.

3 I can talk about things and people important to me.

4 I completed Review 1!

3 Amazing bodies

Let's review! | SB p20–21 ➡ | Find and trace. Then say.

 a
 u
 g

1 Trace and match.

eyes

nose

mouth

ears

arms

legs

hands

feet

Tell me!
Look at my new words. Match and color.

The body

School things

22

Say the words in alphabetical order.

Extra Time?

1   Listen and check (✓).

1

2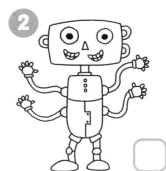

3

4

2 Read and count. Then write.

 **My body**

I have _____2_____ legs.
I have _____ arms.
I have _____ eyes.
I have _____ ears.

 I can shine!

3 🖊 Draw your robot. Write. Then tell a friend.

I have _____
_____
_____.

color me

Write your favorite body word. _____

1 SB p34–35 **Which is the one that doesn't belong? Look and check (✓).**

2 **Find and color. Then circle.**

Let's imagine!

My aunt / grandma / friend can dance.

I can shine!

3 **Draw. Then say.**

And you? Can you dance?

color me

Rate the story and tell a friend. ☆☆☆

Extra Time?

1 Trace. Then read and circle.

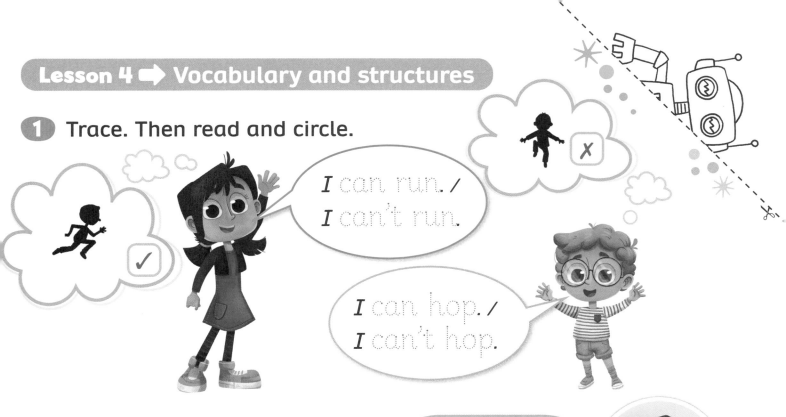

I can run. /
I can't run.

I can hop. /
I can't hop.

2 Look, read, and write.

Let's build!

What can you see?

1 I can hop.   C

2 I can jump.

3 I can dance.

4 I can run.

Think of something you can do. Draw and share with a friend.

Extra Time?

1 (3.13) Listen and check (✓) or put an ✗.

	run	jump	hop	dance
1	✓			
2				

My sounds

2 (3.14) Listen and repeat. Trace. Then match.

m

n

9

I can shine!

3 What can you do? Circle. Then tell a friend.

I *can / can't* jump.

I *can / can't* dance.

I *can / can't* run.

I *can / can't* hop.

color me

1 **Look, read, and number. Then say.**

touch your nose ☐

don't move ☐

close your eyes ☐

clap your hands ☐ 1

1 – Clap your hands!

Think and share

Do you play together with friends? What games?

I can shine!

2 **Trace and write. Then role-play.**

Close your eyes.
Good job!

_____ your _____.
Good job!

_____ your _____.
Good job!

color me

Play a clapping game with a friend.

Extra Time?

1 ✏ Draw and trace. Then color.

I have...

1 mouth.   4 arms.
1 nose.   4 hands.
3 eyes.   3 legs.
6 ears.   3 feet.

2 💬 Match and trace. Then play with a friend.

1

I can dance.

I can run.

I can hop.

I can jump.

2

3

I can run.

4

Elephant.

I have big feet. I'm a dog. I can't __ __ __ __ __ in the story. Who am I? Look at SB pages 34-35.

Extra Time?

3 🖊 ✂ 💬 Stick and check (✓) or put an ✗. Then tell a friend.

You are a robot.
Can you dance?

Yes, I can.

4 Think and write for you. Then ask a friend and write.

	Me	_____
I can ✓		
I can't ✗		

Make an "I can do it!" poster. Then show and tell your family.

Home-school link

29

4 Let's eat up

Lesson 1 ➡ Vocabulary

Let's review! SB p32–33 ➡ Find and write. Then say.

h

1 Trace and match.

bread

milk

chicken

cheese

olives

tomatoes

bananas

strawberries

Tell me!
Look at my new words. Match and color.

a

The body

b

Food

Say the words in alphabetical order.

Extra time?

Lesson 2 ➡ Structures

1 Listen and check (✓) or put an ✗.

1 — ✓ 2 — ☐ 3 — ☐ 4 — ☐

2 🖍 Trace. Then read and draw ☺ or ☹.

 I like *bananas.*

I like *bread.*

I don't like *tomatoes.*

I don't like *chicken.*

1 ☺ **2** ☹ **3** ☹ **4** ☹

 I can shine!

3 🖍 Color the food you like in Activity 2. Write. Then tell a friend.

I like
_____.

color me

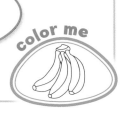

Write your favorite food word. _____

Extra time?

Lesson 3 ➡ Story

1 `SB p44–45` Look and find. Then check (✓) the food you see together.

1  **+**  ☐ **2**  **+**  ☐

3  **+**  ☐

2 🖉 Read and find. Then color.

Let's imagine!
I like cheese and strawberries.

I can shine!

3 🖉 Draw. Then say.

And you? What's your favorite food in school?

color me

Rate the story and tell a friend. ☆☆☆   **Extra time?**

1 Trace. Then look and write.

1 [d] I like sandwiches.   2 [ ] I like pizza.

3 [ ] I don't like milkshakes.   4 [ ] I don't like ice cream.

2 Follow and find. Trace and circle for Elena. Then say.

Let's build!

Ask me questions about food!

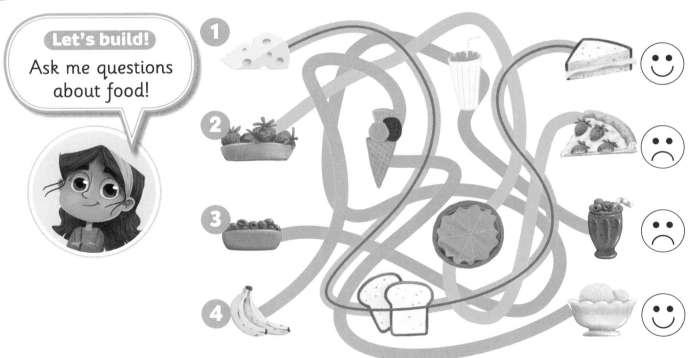

1 Do you like cheese sandwiches?
Yes, I do. / No, I don't.

2 Do you like strawberry pizza?
Yes, I do. / No, I don't.

3 Do you like olive milkshakes?
Yes, I do. / No, I don't.

4 Do you like banana ice cream?
Yes, I do. / No, I don't.

Think of your favorite sandwich. Draw and share with a friend.

Extra Time?

1 🎧 (4.13) Listen and check (✓) or put an ✗.

My sounds

2 🎧 (4.14) ✏ Listen and repeat. Trace. Then color "ch" words blue and "h" words red.

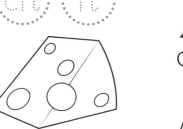   

I can shine!

3 ✏ Circle the food you like. Ask and answer. Then draw for a friend.

My friend's food

My food

bread	milkshakes
tomatoes	sandwiches
pizza	cheese
strawberries	ice cream

Do you like bread?

Yes, I do.

color me

1 Circle four differences. Then say.

1

2

*Picture 1.
Pasta.*

Think and share

Think about when you order food. Do you say "please"?

I can shine!

2 Read and choose three foods. Write. Then role-play.

Menu

milkshakes
strawberries
pizza
pasta
rice
salad
soup
sandwiches
ice cream

Can I have some... , please?

color me

Guess your friend's favorite food.

Extra time?

35

1 ✏️ Read and draw.

> I like cheese and olives. I don't like tomatoes and bananas.

> I like milk and chicken. I don't like strawberries and bread.

2 💬 Trace and match to make your own food. Then ask and answer.

Menu

> Do you like… ?

> Yes, I do./ No, I don't.

1. cheese   ice cream
2. olives   milkshakes
3. bananas   sandwiches
4. strawberries   pizza

What's this? i _ _ _ c _ _ _

Extra time?

3 ✏️ ✂️ 💬 **Stick, draw, and color. Then play the game.**

start →

finish →

I like cheese.

I don't like pizza.

4 **Read. Then think and write.**

Food

At home

In school

At a picnic

_____

_____

_____

_____

_____

_____

_____

_____

4

Make a picnic basket. Then show and tell your family.

Home-school link

Review 2 All about me

1 (4.19) Listen and follow. Then check (✓).

2 Trace. Then look at Activity 1 and match.

1
I like bananas. I like strawberries. I don't like milk.

2
I don't like bananas. I don't like tomatoes. I like chicken.

3 Ask and answer.

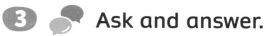

Do you like olives?

Yes, I do.

Do you like cheese?

No, I don't.

4 Look and check (✓) for you. Then role-play.

MENU

Can I have some pizza, please?

5 Trace. Then look and match.

1

I have 4 legs and 2 big ears. I can run.

FACT SHEET

2

I have small eyes. I can hop.

FACT SHEET

Mini-project

6 Think of a pet for you. What can your pet do? Draw and write.

I have _____ and _____.
I can _____.

Time to shine!

7  Read and color.

1 I can write body words.

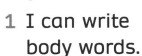

2 I can write food words.

3 I can talk about what I like and have.

4 I completed Review 2!

5 Nature around us

SB p42-43

Lesson 1 ➡ Vocabulary

Let's review!   Find and write. Then say.

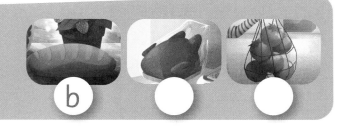

b

1 Look and write.

frog   lizard   mouse   turtle   fox   ~~owl~~   rabbit   duck

_____owl_____

1

2

3

4

5

6

7

8

Tell me! Look at my new words. Match and color.

a

Toys

b

Nature

Extra time? Say the words in alphabetical order.

1  5.06 Listen and check (✓) or put an ✗.

1
2
3
4

✓ ☐ ☐ ☐

2 Trace. Then count and write.

I can see __6__ frogs, _____ rabbits, _____ owls, and _____ lizards.

I can shine!

3 ✏ Draw and write. Then tell a friend.

I can see

_____.

color me

Write your favorite animal word. _____

1 SB p 56–57 ➡ Circle the one that doesn't belong.

1  **2**  **3**  **4**

2 Connect the dots. Then read and circle.

Let's imagine!
I can see an owl / a butterfly.

20
21
• 19
• 6
5
7 •
22 • • 4
23 • • 3
24 • • 2
8 •
9 •
• 18
• 17
16 • 25 • • 1 • 10
13
15 14 12 11

I can shine!

3 🖍 Draw. Then say.

And you? Can you see a big animal?

color me

Rate the story and tell a friend. ☆☆☆

Extra time?

1 **Trace. Then read and circle.**

1 Is it a ladybug? Yes, it is / No, it isn't.

2 Is it a bee? Yes, it is. / No, it isn't.

2 **Follow and find. Then write.**

Let's build!
Which animals are at the park?

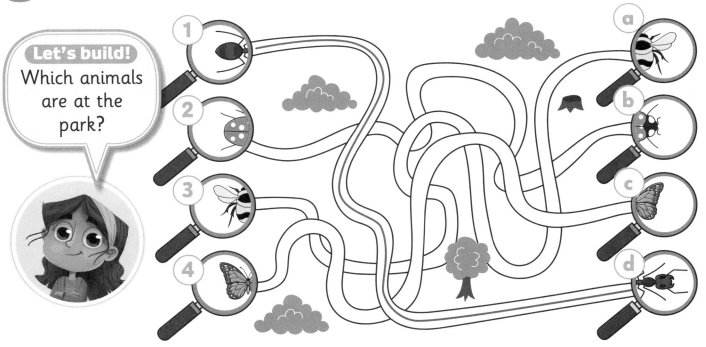

butterfly ~~ant~~ ladybug bee

1 It's a small ___ant___.   **2** It's a red _____.

3 It's a big _____.   **4** It's a blue _____.

Think of your favorite small animal. Draw and share with a friend.

Extra Time?

43

1 🎧 *5.13* **Listen and number.**

My sounds

2 🎧 *5.14* **Listen and repeat. Trace. Then check (✓) the one that doesn't belong.**

I can shine!

3 💬✏️ **Ask and answer with a friend. Then draw.**

Is it a/an... ?

Yes, it is.

color me

1 Read and trace. Check (✓) or put an ✗. Then say.

Look at the frog.

pond

✓

flowers

tree

grass

Think and share

Think about a park close to you. Can you find a pond with ducks or frogs?

I can shine!

2 Choose an animal home and draw an animal in it. Write. Then role-play.

pond   tree

grass   flowers

Look at the _____.
Let's find a _____!

color me

What can you see in your classroom? Tell a friend.

Extra time?

1 **Look. Then count and write.**

| frogs | lizards | ~~mouse~~ | turtles | foxes | owls | rabbits | ducks |

I can see 1 ___mouse___ , 2 _____ , 3 _____ , 4 _____ ,
5 _____ , 6 _____ , 7 _____ , and 8 _____ .

2 **Trace and circle. Draw and write. Then ask and answer.**

Fact Sheet 1

Is it a bee?

No, it isn't.

It's a ladybug / butterfly.

FACT SHEET 2

It's a _____ .

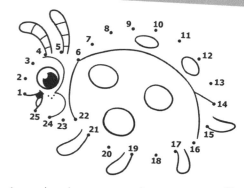

What can you see? I can see a
_ _ _ _ _ _ .

Extra time?

3 ✏️ ✂️ 💬 **Stick and color. Then tell a friend.**

1

I can see one fox.

It's a butterfly.

4 **Read. Then think and write.**

Animals

pond   flowers

tree   grass

Let's dress up

Let's review! SB p54–55 ➡ Find and write. Then say.

d

1 **Look and write.**

shirt   pants   sweater   shoes   dress   shorts   T-shirt   ~~pajamas~~

pajamas

Tell me!
Look at my new words. Match and color.

a

Clothes

b

Nature

Say the words in alphabetical order.

Extra time?

1 🎧 6.06 ✏️ **Listen and color.**

1   2   3   4

2 **Look at Activity 1. Then read and write.**

shoes   ~~shorts~~   pants   shirt

1 I'm wearing purple <u>shorts</u>.

2 I'm wearing black _____.

3 I'm wearing pink _____.

4 I'm wearing a blue _____.

I can shine!

3 **Check (✓) and say. Then tell a friend.**

I'm wearing...

pajamas ☐
a T-shirt ☐   a dress ☐
shoes ☐
pants ☐
a sweater ☐

color me

Write your favorite clothes word. _____

Lesson 3 ➡ Story

1 SB p66–67 **Who is happy? Look and circle.**

2 Find and color.
Then say.

Let's imagine!
I'm wearing a purple sweater/
T-shirt, black shoes, and
blue pants/shorts.

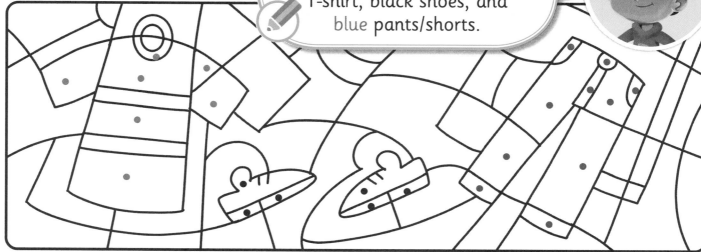

3 Draw and color.
Write for you. Then say.

I'm wearing

_____.

color me

Rate the story and tell a friend. ☆☆☆

Extra time?

1 Trace. Then read and number.

1 I'm hot.

2 I'm happy.

3 I'm sad.

4 I'm cold.

2 Read and write.

Let's build!
What are you wearing?

~~cold~~   hot   sad   happy

1 I'm wearing pajamas. I'm _____cold_____.

2 I'm wearing my favorite dress. I'm _____.

3 I'm wearing two sweaters. I'm _____.

4 I'm wearing a yellow T-shirt. I don't like yellow. I'm

_____. But I have a red jumper. I like red!

Think of your favorite clothes. Draw and share with a friend.

Extra Time?

1 🎧 6.13 **Listen and check (✓).**

① a   b

② a   b

My sounds

2 🎧 6.14 **Listen and repeat. Trace. Then color "j" words blue and "sh" words green.**

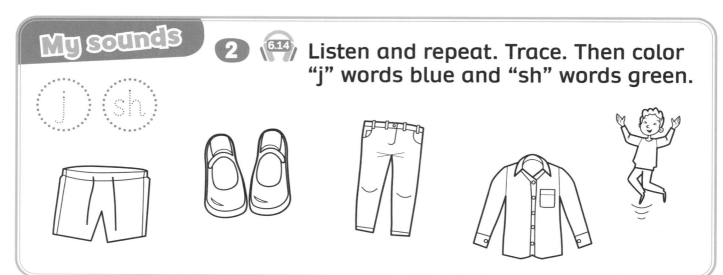

j   sh

I can shine!

3 ✏️ **Color clothes for a cold day. Write. Then tell a friend.**

I'm wearing
_____
and _____ .

color me

1 **Look and write. Then say.**

boots   skirt   hat   ~~jeans~~

1    **2**    **3**    **4**

jeans _____ _____ _____

I'm wearing jeans.

Think and share

Think about a festival. Do you dress up with your friends?

I can shine!

2 🖊 **Draw special clothes for your friend. Write. Then role-play.**

Wear _____ and _____!

color me

What are your favorite special clothes? Tell a friend.

Extra time?

1 Trace and write.

pants	shorts
a shirt	a T-shirt
shoes	pajamas
a dress	a sweater

I'm wearing
<u>a T-shirt</u> ,
_____ ,
and
_____ .

I'm wearing
_____ ,
_____ ,
and
_____ .

2 Trace and match. Then role-play.

 I'm sad.

 I'm hot.

I'm cold.

I'm happy.

54

What's this? It's a __ __ __.

Extra time?

3 Stick, draw, and color. Then play the game.

start

finish

I'm wearing pajamas.

I'm wearing a hat. I'm hot.

4 Read. Then think and write.

My Clothes

Favorite

Special

Make a party hat. Then show and tell your family.

Review 3 — Around me

1 Find and circle five differences.

2 🎧 *6.19* Listen and check (✓).

3 Look at Activity 1. Trace. Then read and number.

> I'm wearing shorts.
> I can see a mouse.

> I'm wearing a dress.
> I can see a lizard.

4 💬 Play *Which picture?* with a friend.

> I'm wearing jeans.
> I can see a frog.

> Is it Picture 2?

> Yes, it is.

5 Trace. Then look and write. | sad   hot   happy |

1

I'm wearing
pajamas.
I'm _____.

2

I'm wearing pants
and a sweater.
I'm _____.

3

I'm wearing
a shirt.
I'm _____.

Mini-project

6 ✏ Draw clothes for your friend's costume party. Then write and say.

I'm wearing _____.
I'm _____.

Time to shine!

7 ✏ Read and color.

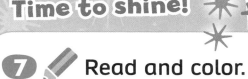

1 I can write animal words.

2 I can write clothes words.

3 I can talk about what's around me.

4 I completed Review 3!

✓ ? ✗

Goodbye from Rise and Shine Towers

1 Trace. Then write and say.

I can see a...

book   pencil   flower   door

tree   bird   bag   ball

School		Park
book	_____	_____
_____	_____	_____
_____		

2 🎧 *7.05* Listen and number.

a

b

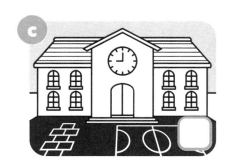

c

3 Trace. Then circle.

It's a school.
I can see books / flowers.

It's a park.
I can see desks / trees.

4 Look and write. Then point, ask, and answer.

Is it a/an… ?

Yes, it is./
No, it isn't.

music box
strawberries
elephant
bird party
rabbit

music box _____ _____

_____ _____ _____

5 Trace. Then sing the Goodbye song.

Goodbye!
Have a great vacation!

It's fall!

1 🎧 8.04 ✏️ Trace and match. Then listen and color.

(tree) (leaf) (apple) (chestnut) (pumpkin) (fire)

Winter vacation

2 🎧 8.08 Trace and match. Then listen and number.

(hat) (gloves) (scarf) (boots) (snow) (lights)

Spring is here!

3 (8.12) Trace. Then listen and number.

⬜ egg | ⬜ blossom | 1 chick | ⬜ lamb | ⬜ flower | ⬜ rabbit

Sunny summer days

4 (8.16) Trace. Then listen and circle.

I'm wearing my
(sun hat) / swimsuit.
I'm wearing a sun hat / sunglasses, too.
All ready to play,
On a sunny / picnic, summer day.

I'm wearing my
swimsuit / sunglasses.
We have a beach / picnic lunch.
Let's have an ice cream each,
And go to the picnic / beach!

Picture Dictionary

Welcome

Vocabulary

 bag

 book

 chair

 desk

 door

 pencil

Unit 1

Vocabulary 1

 ball

 car

 doll

 elephant

 robot

tablet

teddy bear

 train

Vocabulary 2

 big

 new

old

 small

Unit 2

Vocabulary 1

 aunt

 brother

 dad

 grandpa

 grandma

 mom

 sister

 uncle

Vocabulary 2

 bird

 cat

 hamster

 fish

Unit 3

Vocabulary 1

 arms

 ears

 eyes

 feet

 hands

 legs

 mouth

 nose

Vocabulary 2

 dance

 hop

 jump

 run

Unit 4

Vocabulary 1

 bananas

 bread

 cheese

 chicken

 milk

 olives

 strawberries

tomatoes

Vocabulary 2

 ice cream

milkshake

 pizza

 sandwiches

Unit 5

Vocabulary 1

 duck

 fox

 frog

 lizard

 mouse

 owl

 rabbit

 turtle

Vocabulary 2

 ant

 bee

 butterfly

 ladybug

Unit 6

Vocabulary 1

 dress
 sweater
 pajamas
 shirt

 shoes
 shorts
 pants
 T-shirt

Vocabulary 2

 cold
 happy

 hot
 sad

Fall

Vocabulary

 apple
 chestnut
 fire

 leaf
 pumpkin
 tree

Winter

Vocabulary

 boots
 gloves
 hat

 lights
 scarf
 snow

Spring

Vocabulary

 blossom
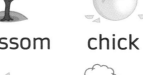 chick
 egg

 flower
 lamb
 rabbit

Summer

Vocabulary

 beach
 picnic
 sunglasses

 sun hat
 sunny
swimsuit